ALMOST HUMAN

A PREPONDERANCE OF
APHORISMS TO PONDER

DAVID L. LAING

Cosmic Art Center

Published in the United States of America

Cosmic Art Center
62 Cedar St.
Apt. 601
Seattle, Washington 98121

Paperback ISBN: 978-1-960089-04-5

CONTENTS

APHORISM

a concise statement of a principle;
a terse formulation of a truth or sentiment

—Merriam-Webster Dictionary

FOREWORD

What good is a world that cannot be improved by Imagination?

That's aphorism number 798 in this book. It could well be
David L. Laing's personal motto. His imagination never
stops generating images and ideas. Often that boundless
creativity manifests as drawings, sometimes as articles,
occasionally as novels.

Most recently, thousands of aphorisms have gushed forth,
enough to fill many books. This is the second. The series
began with aphorisms 1 to 750 in *Not Yet Human*. This volume
contains aphorisms 751 to 1500. *Just Human* and *Fully Human*
are forthcoming, each with another 750 aphorisms, and
several more aphorism books are in the works!

David's aphorisms may be metaphors or conundrums, wise
or humorous. They are presented not by theme or concept,
nor grouped in any order, just poured out as they sprang to

David's mind. As in his books of articles, the *Beyond the Box* series, the organization is randomness.

The 750 aphorisms in each volume are meant to be pondered, as their shared subtitle expresses, rather than devoured in a gulp. Again, we urge you to take your time here. Dip in now and then. Ponder, reflect, contemplate.

Come back again later for a few more gems. There are more to come.

ALMOST HUMAN

APHORISMS

—751—

For the blind, color is sound.

—752—

The *word* contains the entire bird.

—753—

Pain of pure beauty elevates the brain.

—754—

Resolve, solve, evolve.

—755—

Present, past and future
are three sides of a triangle.

—756—

With no dome the room is doomed.

—757—

Dig a hole to unbury oneself whole.

1

—758—

A bit of grit made a pearl then went to bed.

—759—

Make those pay
who hold the spirit of play at bay.

—760—

It is not philosophy
when difficult becomes a cult.

—761—

The only logic to logic is logic.

—762—

Bow and *life* have the same word
in ancient Greek: *bios.*

—763—

Penchant for wordplay; we chant it all day.

—764—

Logos is a word that means the "Word."

—765—

Truth is in the proportion
of the bounding line.

—766—

Create fate.

—767—

Not only ale grows stale.

—768—

Peace of mind: unify warring opposites.

—769—

Confuse that mere fragment for the whole
and the piece is not at peace with itself.

—770—

The greatest find in nature is a mature mind.

—771—

Right path is followed by a river swath.

—772—

Whether going up or down,
it is the same elevator.

—773—

The mountain does not
look down on the valley.

—774—

Are you the *One* to understand yourself?

—775—

God as a notion is in perpetual motion.

—776—

Planets whirl, stars fall—
later, meteors rise from their crater.

—777—

A lie cannot stand.

—778—

Cannot avoid the void.

—779—

Play and pray to not become the prey.

—780—

There is no river to step into,
only its meander to draw form and from.

—781—

All things are one,
even though they are not.

—782—

Few have the strength to go the length.

—783—

If you don't do the steps
there is no stairway.

—784—

A life sentence has its choice—
active or passive voice.

—785—

Doom is no room in the room.

—786—

A city blinded by electricity
is in constant blackout.

—787—

Stars steer their own light chariot.

—788—

The Milky Way:
down by day and gown by night.

—789—

A frieze does not freeze— it frees.

—790—

Depending on depth and belief,
a relief sculpture can bring relief.

—791—

Self determines a giant or an elf.

—792—

Happiness, like a woman,
does not want to be hotly pursued.

—793—

Tour the contour to arrive at the soul.

—794—

Drugs did not need me.

—795—

Symbol is its own bell to chime when it is time.

—796—

Tree Knowledge lives on the edge.

—797—

The body of work has legs.

—798—

What good is a world
that cannot be improved by Imagination?

—799—

Truth is spark, not axiom.

—800—

Inner pressure is the unsung treasure.

—801—

Gouache is never gauche.

—802—

The race of gods has no finish line.

—803—

Did Giants make the world,
or did the world make up giants?

—804—

Durability of the plate
makes the engraving worth saving.

—805—

Take it for granted—
cease to be enchanted.

—806—

The state of the ship is not the ship of state.

—807—

A college is a collage.

—808—

Abstraction is mere distraction.

—809—

Though Baroque began with a flaw,
it became its own law.

—810—

Courtly art has its own ruling.

—811—

With no enemy in sight,
the militaristic spirit attacks its own might.

—812—

Make a difference
through action and indifference.

—813—

Happiness is not to hate one's fate.

—814—

It is all Greek to me—
the language God learned to speak.

—815—

Speak your mind to conceal who you are.

—816—

Forsake knowledge for its own sake.

—817—

How do you know
you are not a life boat from a shipwreck?

—818—
Head in the right direction,
not knowing where you are going.

—819—
The world steals from those
who think for themselves.

—820—
More books, the less read—
less said, the more read.

—821—
Encircle God to be encompassed.

—822—
Certainty turns doubt into a god.

—823—
Appreciate influences fate.

—824—
Wars are waged not only for food
but to be in a good mood.

—825—
Only the head considers God dead.

—826—
God is reinvented just like we are.

—827—

Intent creates content.

—828—

It is not what they say, but how they play.

—829—

A hill is a thrill,
a mountain is a fountain.

—830—

Brains contain their own key and chains.

—831—

There is a piece of everything in everything,
as well as nothing in nothing.

—832—

My kingdom for wisdom.
Is there a difference?

—833—

Is happiness unworthy of us, or we of it?

—834—

In a prison of happiness, sadness is key.

—835—

To perceive or not perceive
is the ultimate question to receive.

—836—

God of gray is an ambiguous actor every day.

—837—

I spin, therefore I'm in.

—838—

Passion is not fashion, it is fashioned.

—839—

We have a lot to say
about what we do not know.

—840—

Strive to *bee* the head of God—a hive.

—841—

Stretch an arm, create a galaxy.

—842—

The psyche is the bridge
between physics and metaphysics.

—843—

The difference between knowledge and belief is
one you believe you know
and the other you know you believe.

—844—

A mortal *can* travel through a portal.

—845—

Trust the senses to make sense *and* nonsense.

—846—

Key and prison are a personal decision.

—847—

Valley of depression cannot compete
with peak-experience expression.

—848—

Grow an arm, cultivate a handful.

—849—

Plant the eyes, harvest spies.

—850—

With legs, farming is disarming.

—851—

A storm is a drop in ecstasy.

—852—

A bosque is a mosque.

—853—

Who is crying when you weep in the rain?

—854—

Train is trained to stay on track.

—855—

To finish, women furnish garnish.

—856—

Everything is water soluble in a solution.

—857—

True form is the bird's-eye view as norm.

—858—

Are the "Forms" God
or is it just an outline to inform?

—859—

Triangle made mountain and snake
to deliver river.

—860—

We all may imagine
the shape of the Universe to be a sphere,
yet it may be a spiral,
a man, or even a box that went viral.

—861—

Mood is in the wood.

—862—

Born old, spend the rest of life
to become young and bold.

—863—
The relationship
between body and soul is whole.

—864—
Peace is the missing piece.

—865—
The Horse of Troy is a grown-up toy
containing all present and future course.

—866—
Choice was made
between carnation and car nation.

—867—
Demiurge is mover and shaker
as well as intellect maker.

—868—
Condemned to a long sentence,
the voice chose adjective—
there to embellish the passive and the active.

—869—
Confined to a *cell,*
the only escape is through a mem*brain.*

—870—

Fraught and self-taught,
fought for freedom in thought.

—871—

Original browser was a drowser.

—872—

Dream upstream where fish return as a team.

—873—

Alpha male tells the tallest tale.

—874—

Sky writing is done on the fly.

—875—

Knowledge from the aliens
is called alienation—
a nation of knowledge seekers as vacation.

—876—

On a roll the scribe completely copied the scroll.

—877—

Unmoored, the Mind sailed for more.

—878—

The bore does not know what to ignore.

—879—
The novel is the new wheel
that got the imagination rolling what to feel.

—880—
Male takes its toll, female pays its fee—
join together to call toll free.

—881—
Cosmic gastronomy is light
being served and swallowed up everywhere.

—882—
Frightened is unenlightened.

—883—
Regardless of age, mind can be compared
to an effervescent beverage—
think, drink and be drunk
from what is in its treasured trunk.

—884—
Taste victory from its back story.

—885—
Dream of mouth downstream
and source upstream
or swim with the current majority
in mediocrity.

—886—

The head is the ultimate book to be read.

—887—

Sage dies to live again at another age.

—888—

The human being became discontent
when its form lost content.

—889—

Creative ability increases active security.

—890—

Become accidental and mortal
with no glimpse through the portal.

—891—

Quality trumps duality.

—892—

Mind is inexhaustible farmland
to follow and not lay fallow.

—893—

Take off the coat to cross the moat,
draw from the bridge to the picture boat.

—894—

Good sense includes nonsense.

—895—

Molded by thoughts, sculpture in rapture.

—896—

The world is a nervous system tired
and the nervous system a world hard wired.

—897—

Imprisoned by the world or its word.

—898—

Fear of failure is the allure of the spear.

—899—

Search for the end and the beginning
in the middle where virtue lies.

—900—

Hold what we behold.

—901—

A cloud is a droplet shroud.

—902—

Forgetting it was a fountain,
inhabit its mountain.

—903—

Nose of the rose is the thorn in scent reborn.

—904—

Dew does what it do.

—905—

Altitude in attitude and attitude in altitude.

—906—

What kind of mind is mankind?

—907—

Cannot belittle and live large.

—908—

Handle a candle—name its flame.

—909—

If a tree can produce paper,
then paper can introduce a tree.

—910—

Gentle is strength's mantle.

—911—

An archer is a sharp teacher.

—912—

Truth is heard from a whisper, not a whistle.

—913—

An eagle knows not to imitate crows.

—914—

Leave footprints not fingerprints.

—915—

Each of the five fingers
is a dimension to have a hand in.

—916—

Know a god by becoming one.

—917—

Plants speak well-founded
getting to the root of an issue well-grounded.

—918—

Appear as the spear, hurled and unfurled.

—919—

Be glad you are mad—not angry.

—920—

Luck is to call a friend and find a fortune.

—921—

God's present is presence.

—922—

Trained to not see,
you don't know when you are free.

—923—
Not in pursuit,
the forest gives all rest and fruit.

—924—
A leaf is its own sheath.

—925—
Inside out, upside down,
lying, standing, asleep or awake—
you are what you make.

—926—
Unmute to transmute.

—927—
Got a letter from God
with no return address—lives everywhere.

—928—
Walking is feet talking.

—929—
Sixth sense makes the most sense.

—930—
Dance to enhance chance.

—931—
No facts, only acts.

—932—

The priest *is* the feast.

—933—

Mode of perception is code of imagination.

—934—

Arcane is its own plane.

—935—

Symbols do not clash.

—936—

Bend the universe to blend its verse.

—937—

The rope is not its knot.

—938—

The celestial angle of the angel is right.

—939—

Secret abode is an angel's code.

—940—

When we wing it, we help angels sing it.

—941—

Too invisible to visualize size.

—942—

Recast the fishing net to catch the cast.

—943—

Trust protects against rust.

—944—

The deed can feed the need.

—945—

The boomerang did not begin with a bang,
yet returned as it sang.

—946—

Became the name from where you came.

—947—

Philosophy and religion are separated by region.

—948—

An insect is a perfect six-legged sect.

—949—

A spider has eight reasons
to put its own spin on a web.

—950—

Art is where belief can start.

—951—
Number awakened the world from slumber—
a spacial extension to remember.

—952—
Knowing will toil to keep the oil flowing.

—953—
To get the right angle of the triangle—
try a new angle.

—954—
A lot of ink is spent
to be content with right content.

—955—
Creativity versus neurosis—
it is the only choice in crisis.

—956—
Self-division does not add up.

—957—
Toil for the right to mortal foil.

—958—
It's irrational to dismiss irrational.

—959—
The vision of a new cloud shape is not clouded.

—960—

Over-arching hierarchy is not anarchy.

—961—

All in Mind—Mind in All.

—962—

A pear is never alone.

—963—

The spine is the pineal's pine—a cone of one.

—964—

In vein but not in vain,
the heart pumped up to the brain.

—965—

Each brain lobe together
is the globe covered by a green robe.

—966—

The brain is the membrane,
said the "*mighty*chondia."

—967—

Well-being is deep.

—968—

The humming bird has no time to sing.

—969—

Higher Glyphs came from the Upper Nile.

—970—

Hieroglyph was the last time
image and word played the same riff.

—971—

The Nile has a serpentine profile.

—972—

The circle has it covered by surrounding itself.

—973—

Is there a reason why know sounds like *no?*

—974—

Yes is the best guess.

—975—

The trio of etudes includes:
aptitude, altitude and attitude.

—976—

The book took the hook—
the head became well-read—
the brain cut its teeth
on hard words well-punctuated.

—977—

Need the stomach of a sage to digest the page.

—978—

In a rowboat there are two choices:
either oar.

—979—

Evolve needs something to solve.

—980—

Canoe is the sun ray's shoe.

—981—

It was a boon,
switching heads with the moon.

—982—

The cloud accompanies the lightning flash
thundering loud.

—983—

Reign of rain covers its plain.

—984—

Invisible hand counts each grain of sand.

—985—

Greater the force— closer the source.

—986—

Flash of insight— clash of lightning bright.

—987—

Insecurity is not secure with maturity.

—988—

"I'd" is not real, it's an *ide*al.

—989—

Hypnogogic is the other side of logic.

—990—

Down the straight path
flies a curve ball for all.

—991—

When you *pick* the guitar,
there are strings attached.

—992—

Always toiled never spoiled.

—993—

With no patron the painter is pure neuron.

—994—

If you follow the Nile,
voluntary exile is good for a while.

—995—

Content, not form, will be the future norm.

—996—

Creativity produces—madness reduces.

—997—

Wisdom is showing growing—
not showing knowing.

—998—

The polymath follows a jolly path
doing it all, including math.

—999—

Going forward or reverse,
the universe is verse.

—1000—

One thousand reasons
you can't control weather of the seasons.

—1001—

Seven years in a foreign land
is the span to form a new man.

—1002—

Kingdom collapsed due to boredom.

—1003—
Discover Zen through laughter of the pen.

—1004—
Discipline is the palate cleanser
for an evolutionary diet.

—1005—
What you cannot say, you write—
what you cannot write
is swallowed by the night.

—1006—
Labor suits its fruits.

—1007—
Trees self-nourish to flourish.

—1008—
Nothing heard to follow the herd.

—1009—
Jest and zest for the quest.

—1010—
Genes of a genius are another genre.

—1011—
With thoughts of grain
wind plants in the plain.

—1012—

Lunar and solar,
the yin and yang of all knowledge circular.

—1013—

Oar is stroked to soar.

—1014—

Create outside with inside.

—1015—

A "peak experience"
is a peek at the light of height
and the height of light.

—1016—

Rhyme to remind the mind to have a good time.

—1017—

To be active and conductive
is either expansive or reductive.

—1018—

We draw up our happiness from well-being.

—1019—

We are what we do and do what we are.

—1020—

What is power through fear and the spear,
compared to the chain of hammer,
anvil and stirrup of the inner ear?

—1021—

Earth form sculpted by the worm.

—1022—

Each body part is its own art.

—1023—

Train the brain mode to explain the code.

—1024—

Create your own provenance—
originate a world.

—1025—

No praise in the modernity malaise.

—1026—

Woman as dam—electric waterfall for all.

—1027—

What seems out there is actually in here.

—1028—

Serious jest plays best in the love nest.

—1029—

Moral code is an oral mode.

—1030—

Mental state opens physical gate.

—1031—

The mantra "om" is in c*om*e and h*om*e.

—1032—

The origin of the world
imitated a poetic language of natural order.

—1033—

The generation of the universe
put forth in the language of verse.

—1034—

An over abundance of meaning
can be demeaning
in the "sense of purpose" dance.

—1035—

Divinity is in the vicinity.

—1036—

Intellect alone is alone— not one.

—1037—
Do the math;
the body is composed of
more than one path.

—1038—
In an alphabetical cosmology
letters structure the derivation of all things.

—1039—
If men were birds and birds were men,
the world would be one infinite nest
where after all labor was done
would be there to rest.

—1040—
Transcend has no end— only where to begin.

—1041—
No one paid the Cosmic Egg to be laid—
the catch was made before anything could hatch.

—1042—
Passively established way of perception
is not an actively bright form of conception.

—1043—
The actor is the character,
but the character is *not* the actor.

—1044—

Ecstasy occurs when a certain thought eclipses
and exponentially adds to another.

—1045—

Cosmology is pure gastronomy
with light being served
and swallowed up everywhere.

—1046—

You are on the right path
when the river follows *you.*

—1047—

The universe is already granulated
in a grain of sand to see itself.

—1048—

Prior to the coming of perspective
the world was introspective.

—1049—

Whatever reaches further has more reality.

—1050—

Drawing a conclusion—withdrawing an illusion.

—1051—

A stream of zeros makes pools
that evolve into mathematical schools.

—1052—

A row of boats ready to row.

—1053—

A flexible world bends to a new word.

—1054—

Milky Way can drape
another light cape as cloak night.

—1055—

Intuition is direct insight into the night.

—1056—

The most reliable staff is the one you walk with.

—1057—

Corral the stars to plant new planets.

—1058—

All prisoners and zebras have in common
is their stripes.

—1059—

Fail to find the grail—
choose palace over chalice.

—1060—

No mantra, no tantra.

— 1061 —

Rainbow is waterfall's resurrection show.

— 1062 —

Synchronicities more frequently appear
when optimism is near.

— 1063 —

Behold the world—
see an original origami unfold.

— 1064 —

Pleasure to seek a sneak peak—
treasure to search for a feature peak.

— 1065 —

Wages are stages down through the ages.

— 1166 —

Utterance is circular advance
in a poetical rhyme dance.

— 1067 —

If the bird were a plane,
flight would be a light plan.

— 1068 —

Handle man as a candle to enlighten—
not manhandle.

—1069—
Sum of what you imagine
to become some.

—1070—
What we behold we hold as it holds us.

—1071—
Train a tree with rain.

—1072—
Difference between active
and passive is massive.

—1073—
Individuate is to graduate.

—1074—
Inferiority is passive; superiority is active.

—1075—
Canoe of the shoe walks on water.

—1076—
The "blind spot"
is the source of *true vision* caught.

—1077—
The universe is more real
in the magical half-light of the candle-lit night.

—1078—
Do not fail to sail
out of one world into another.

—1079—
In an historic flash
the meteor makes epic splash.

—1080—
Cosmic and comic
are separated only by *S* for sonic.

—1081—
The ultimate flying carpet
is a pen and paper target.

—1082—
Visionary vitality rivals triviality.

—1083—
A certain kind of disaster
leads to better things faster.

—1084—
The treat is we are our own retreat.

—1085—
Protecting the Mind as living proof,
the roof of Superconsciousness is no spoof.

—1086—
If it sincerely comes from within,
there is no sin.

—1087—
To make fantasy real could be a fantastic deal.

—1088—
Without those sudden bursts of *newness*
the valleys become deeper
than the peaks are high.

—1089—
Bubbling in the brew
are things you now *see* and always knew.

—1090—
Mind is the site of the mental parasite—
its key insight is to kill its rite.

—1091—
Science of the past—magic of the future.

—1092—
More lion than iron
is the man of the wheel not steel.

—1093—
Jest points towards zest from east to west.

—1094—
The universe planted in space
grew from a seed to create a race.

—1095—
The rowboat is no robot.

—1096—
The sage will turn the next page of a future age.

—1097—
Know something about nothing
and nothing about something.

—1098—
The key to the kingdom
is the paradoxical nature of freedom.

—1099—
Boarding the boat-of-imagination is not boring.

—1100—
Evolution is seeing the depths
where others see only the sea.

—1101—
A hammer with a stammer
will fail to find the nail.

—1102—

World on the brink will become what we think.

—1103—

Euphoric needs to be ouroboric.

—1104—

With wings for windows
and a long neck for the main door,
the temple took off air-borne
leaving its ground floor.

—1105—

Sailfish and swordfish
are two philosophers—
each with its own theory
for thought and action.

—1106—

Shark and lark
disagreed upon the usage of the ark.

—1107—

Infinity is played infinitely.

—1108—

Wo*man* contains man within.

—1109—

Pleasure is a sure plea for more pressure.

—1110—

The head is an egg
and the body is rooted underground
for both bird and plant to hatch and abound.

—1111—

In the end, pay to have something to say.

—1112—

Ancient gods had a bow
and made rain before the rainbow.

—1113—

Without internal light
outside would be eternal night:
behold the threshold.

—1114—

Heaven owes more to *become* than to *be*.

—1115—

Only difference between inner and outer
is reference.

—1116—

Trust wanderlust more, as one must.

—1117—

Believe that Imagination's
"make-believe" is real.

—1118—

Maintain the unity conserved—
become the observed.

—1119—

Where knowledge stops, imagination begins.

—1120—

Turn imagination into rings of Saturn.

—1121—

Knowledge is the wire;
Imagination is its current on fire.

—1122—

Cosmetically make up the face;
beautify unfinished cosmic space.

—1123—

One terse verse of the story of the Universe
written to move forward, not reverse.

—1124—

If the head is a book page,
the body a boat and the heart an anchor,
then to sail what is written cannot fail.

—1125—

Unseen Force is the world source.

—1126—
That which explains
cannot be part of the *explained*—
it remains outside the *ride.*

—1127—
What dark matter is to the visible universe,
the unconscious mind is to the conscious.

—1128—
Creativity of the hands
helps the artist conquer unseen lands.

—1129—
Become a ladder to not get sadder.

—1130—
The world of knife and strife
is forever ranging and ever changing.

—1131—
The more the mind
tries to "civilize" wilderness,
the wilder it becomes.

—1132—
Brain-washed to perfection—
God is a clean deal.

—1133—

How to slow it down in a hurry.

—1134—

Never born a blank slate
with nothing on the plate.

—1135—

Passivity is the habitual activity of an entire city.

—1136—

God is a membrane
between the will to create and a plane
where only truth can permeate.

—1137—

Illumination can handle
the flame of the candle.

—1138—

Make no mistake, the Mind is a cratered lake.

—1139—

Dig, dig, dig, till done—
that hole *is* you—whole.

—1140—

Escape from prison in a magic cape—
a caper of an escapade suddenly made.

—1141—

The *robot* robs you of life
by doing the job too well—
a slacker would be preferable to this hacker.

—1142—

Become the cape of God—
escape in a merry pod.

—1143—

Believe in what you create, not innate fate.

—1144—

Improve one's self image
with the help of the mage.

—1145—

Books fall like rain
to make plants rise to the brain.

—1146—

Ether is either here or there— ethe*real.*

—1147—

Egypt is cryptic.

—1148—

The internal dream moves up the seam.

—1149—

The *leap-of-faith*
is both physical and psychological.

—1150—

Tulips have two red lips.

—1151—

A poet, writer and artist
know less what they are doing
than a philosopher, yet get more done.

—1152—

The Universe is an unfinished work of art
that still needs us to do our part.

—1153—

The ultimate battle will be fought
in the field of aesthetics.

—1154—

The rise of the novel did more
to change the mind, imagination and history
than the fall of the hypocrisy of aristocracy.

—1155—

Aristocracy of the spirit is a fine line,
not bloodline.

—1156—

The fool sees consciousness as clearly as a pool.

—1157—

Epiphanies come to young and bolder,
symphonies for older to shoulder.

—1158—

Power is grace in space.

—1159—

Boxed in, the argument turned circular.

—1160—

Pair of opposites attract or attack the air.

—1161—

Love envies the glove.

—1162—

You cannot fly in the same sky twice.

—1163—

Having so many sides
baffled all geometrical guides.

—1164—

Reinvent—live out and outside content.

—1165—

Why write what you know?
We know nothing! Write about that!

—1166—

Ultimate drug line is adrenaline.

—1167—

Existentialism: capable of coming up
with meaning and sense of purpose every moment,
and more importantly, on your own.

—1168—

Laugh with the whole heart
to create the ultimate food of the mood.

—1169—

Some *hand* is the truth of handsome.

—1170—

Body is also author and composer—
it writes in space—both single and double.

—1171—

A face is a hologram of the space of who I am.

—1172—

Inside the human trunk
is a spare tire for when we tire
and a jack to raise up the spirit out of its funk.

—1173—

Bodily symmetry is asymmetrical.

—1174—

The hands weren't just handed out filled
but came with untilled lands.

—1175—

A man falls like rain
to irrigate a field chosen for his plain.

—1176—

Don't plod through the sod—plow it with a nod.

—1177—

Conquered a kingdom
through imagination and wisdom.

—1178—

Serpentine and sensual
the river is bathed in, swum in and drunk from.

—1179—

To not think is to think.

—1180—

Paint by number,
faint into slumber in its penumbra.

—1181—
Like the stars,
our light will take years to reach ears.

—1182—
Color of the eyes is reflected in the skies.

—1183—
Grade is how deep can be dug with the spade.

—1184—
The word knows what is coming
an instant before you do.

—1185—
Fig from the *ficus religiosa* is the ultimate gig.

—1186—
Intuition ignition is pattern recognition.

—1187—
Key to forward movement is sideways.

—1188—
A book is both hook and bait,
well worth the wait.

—1189—
A *cast* knew how to fish.

—1190—

Avantgarde guards the future advance
from invasion of the past.

—1191—

The birthplace of the face
has a second coming to grace.

—1192—

Involve, resolve, evolve.

—1193—

Body as seed needs imagination to breed.

—1194—

Real civilization is collective realization.

—1195—

An artist's goal is to be ahead of its time
to have a good time.

—1196—

Nose is the centerpiece
for countenance to compose.

—1197—

A nose for beauty finds the right face to repose.

—1198—

Tired is not hard-wired.

—1199—

By yourself in many— yet at one.

—1200—

Distraction is the devil's invention
and private business transaction.

—1201—

Intuitive insight not turned into art
is missing its main part.

—1202—

New day, new *play.*

—1203—

Arctic tern sees overall pattern.

—1204—

Weakness feeds weakness—
strength breeds strength.

—1205—

Arise to the legacy: the fall is a fallacy.

—1206—

Garbage men are the philosophers of their age;
they earn their cash
emptying other people's trash.

—1207—

Vitality of a natural enthusiast
radiates from far future to distant past.

—1208—

Everything is a mask for all one could ask.

—1209—

Fear of entanglement
is now quantum entertainment.

—1210—

Anatomy is body astronomy compacted
into the high gravity of spatial cavity.

—1211—

Pronounce everything seen all at once.

—1212—

There are no banks to save the stream of time.

—1213—

If all conflict between the sexes were resolved,
their existence would be absolved.

—1214—

There is no striving lost in the living.

—1215—

Logos contains both pathos and chaos.

—1216—

For every bow there is a flaming arrow to throw
and a target to know.

—1217—

Converse animates the universe.

—1218—

The fig leaf cannot hide the fruit of its pursuit.

—1219—

God's footprint is root imprint.

—1220—

Might is light.

—1221—

The midwife to a genius is both love and strife.

—1222—

The idea of the mold is more valuable than gold.

—1223—

A muscle must be strong to outlast a week.

—1224—

Art is the most difficult of all professions
because no one knows
what to do nor how to start.

—1225—

Au revoir to fatigue—connect to God reservoir.

—1226—

Writing raises a sail—
launch to sea to conquer or fail.

—1227—

Harmony creates charm, not harm—
true money.

—1228—

Admonish or astonish—it is a choice to finish.

—1229—

A god needs a man to manifest—
a man needs a god for a festival.

—1230—

A philosopher is a porpoise with a purpose.

—1231—

Oceanic time is not measured in hours and days
but in currents and waves.

—1232—

It's a feat for a shoe to fit the right foot,
let alone the left.

—1233—
A tunnel is a light funnel.

—1234—
Know a man's laughter
and you know what he is after.

—1235—
Mood induces what it produces.

—1236—
On top of the world,
seated on the North Pole,
guided by the North Star,
how could anything go south?

—1237—
There is a "no vacancy" sign
outside the hotel of the human mind,
full of unwanted guests.

—1238—
Thought alone is not enough
to dig up the right bone.

—1239—
Language is its own gauge
without limiting it to an age.

—1240—
Mystical acts, spiritual facts,
are what ultimately attracts.

—1241—
The world is it in a state of flux and flow,
more than we know.

—1242—
Plea of the sea behaves in waves.

—1243—
There is a heart in the head
and a head in the heart—
feel thinking and think feeling.

—1244—
Pleasure, for sure, is a plea for something to cure.

—1245—
Fortunately the rose can never remove
its tinted glasses as head instructor
of flowering classes.

—1246—
To value is to possess— to possess is to devalue.

—1247—
Spiritual beings live their own story—
not sensory.

—1248—
Everything for the one and nothing for the n*one.*

—1249—
Plug the leak— experience the peak.

—1250—
Hallucinate about the *gate*—
open it not up to debate.

—1251—
Inner light is out of sight.

—1252—
There is no mass to happiness.
The adapted formula
from Einstein's $E=mc^2$ is $E=C$.
Energy equals Light.

—1253—
Follow its own law
to fly on a magic carpet— no flaw.

—1254—
There are those who love to live
and those who live to love—
and those who do neither of the above.

—1255—

The moon was a stowaway
on the sun boat's ray.

—1256—

Sighting Atlantis from the mast
of the crow's nest of the past is blest.

—1257—

Twilight and dawn are bookends
of how the daily page transcends.

—1258—

When the gods shower, it rains down power.

—1259—

Sage left only a half a page, yet defined an age.

—1260—

The *palm* tree is a giant hand free.

—1261—

You pass time as time passes you.

—1262—

A pen rows, an oar writes, the book flows.

—1263—

The path is both myth and pith.

—1264—

Bone never *sees* itself as one,
but part of a skeleton—
its marrow is for now and tomorrow.

—1265—

See the god, paint the saint.

—1266—

Force is in full contact with its source—
both circle and cycle.

—1267—

Innocence is sense *and* nonsense
with no pretense.

—1268—

The most dangerous
and difficult "sport" is improvisation—
most who try, abort.

—1269—

Psychedelics showcase ancient relics.

—1270—

Urge to create is greater than fate.

—1271—

How is it this cabal of mediocrities
passes judgment on this hall
of talented eccentricities?

—1272—

Building a raft with no roof is proof of his craft.

—1273—

Trained to express itself,
the express train stays on track.

—1274—

Research is search again for yourself.

—1275—

Compressed, god is in man,
expressed, man is in god.

—1276—

Think between inside and outside
is the missing link.

—1277—

Design a sign not to be heard by the herd
is a good sign.

—1278—

A man of his times is already outdated.

—1279—

The ideal spot for a fire place is in the mind space.

—1280—

Comedy and tragedy are so closely related
that each appears to be a mockery of the other.

—1281—

Hammer an anvil, truth will unveil.

—1282—

A mountain moves of its own accord,
is both faith and lord.

—1283—

Light the dawn, the "higher self" comes to spawn.

—1284—

Roundness of the universe
and the human head are both boundless.

—1285—

To draw draws its own law.

—1286—

What people have most in common
is uncommon.

—1287—

Pressure is what turns a faint line into treasure.

—1288—

Ears, in name of space, frame the face.

—1289—

Symbol contains the circle "o."

—1290—

A world order is never ordered.

—1291—

Does the river flow in us, or do we flow in it?

—1292—

A lake can make no mistake
caught in this gigantic dish of the wish of a fish.

—1293—

A philosopher is a strange mixture
of madness, comedy and purity.

—1294—

Noble man has a mobile hand.

—1295—

Art of medicine embraces all arts
with humor in healing parts.

—1296—

Sun's nom de plume is "Light."

—1297—
Progress comes in small steps,
regress is large leaps.

—1298—
A full mind welcomes an empty house;
an empty mind welcomes a full house.

—1299—
Today a culture does not grow organically
like bacteria, but is manufactured
to not spread on its own.

—1300—
Uncover the hood of manhood.

—1301—
Noted in the notebook are noted musical notes.

—1302—
Door to a far celestial temple
is a five-pointed star.

—1303—
Music is *read* by dancing.

—1304—
Dog is body guard, cat is body god.

—1305—

We are nothing vibrating, which is something.

—1306—

Destiny is a grand cycle
when ridden on a bicycle.

—1307—

Awaken each day in play.

—1308—

No room for gloom in a room of doom.

—1309—

The two greatest systems
are the nervous and the blood.

—1310—

With no dance suffer from a fallacy
of insignificance.

—1311—

A grand fusion can end
this state of total confusion.

—1312—

Was the universe ready-made
or did God make it ready?

—1313—

Ignite the night with light finite.

—1314—

It is not what you do with your talents,
but what they do with you.

—1315—

The descendent lives to inform its transcendent.

—1316—

A member of the Universe can remember verse.

—1317—

The only universal present is present.

—1318—

Wild gaiety is its own satiety.

—1319—

Gods need seed pods and seed pods need gods.

—1320—

There is not only a "leap of faith,"
but also of time, space and grace.

—1321—

Even though a perfect cube is not an elastic tube,
everything else is easy to include.

—1322—

At what point does one become slave
and the other free?

—1323—

Empower the disempowered
to intellectually flower.

—1324—

Freed depends only on creed and greed.

—1325—

We have a minimum knowledge of Maximus.

—1326—

Hammer is good, anvil is evil.
God is the blacksmith.

—1327—

The difference between an umpire
and an emperor is the first can call up all strikes
and the second can strike down all he likes.

—1328—

True scripture is to imbue rapture.

—1329—

Have your cake and eat it two.

—1330—

Getting better is better than being better.

—1331—

A mystery is not reasonable,
reason contains no mystery.

—1332—

Trust August, remember November,
yet begotten with the tune of June.

—1333—

Heiress of the unicorn is uniqueness reborn.

—1334—

A bonfire is a saint's final attire.

—1335—

Heartstrings and pursestrings
have different tunings.

—1336—

Capstone and cornerstone are one and done.

—1337—

Maidenhead made gold out of lead.

—1338—

Paint a saint to feel no pain in the brain.

—1339—

Measure one's weight
hopping a train car of freight.

—1340—

You drank the wine but *it* got drunk.

—1341—

The mountain encircled the mind
and extended its range.

—1342—

Earth found its own cosmic way
of silk without milk.

—1343—

Hemingway and lemmings way were the same.

—1344—

The only river that flows upstream is the dream.

—1345—

The flying fish is the ultimate wish.

—1346—

A coward cannot move forward.

—1347—

You can handle it if it touches you.

—1348—

Imagination creates a nation.

—1349—

The shepherd at one with the herd is heard.

—1350—

Madness and reason—the clue and the glue.

—1351—

All are here for a season—
even the mad without *reason*.

—1352—

Seven roads traveling together
lead to heavenly abodes.

—1353—

More discomfort is comfort
to defend a strong fort—
more secure is dangerous for sure.

—1354—

In the universe room,
the tail of a celestial bird is the ideal broom
that must sweep the cosmic corners
full of star dust.

—1355—

Aghast at the past, there is no future
without being present at last.

—1356—

Discover the rules of the game by *playing*.

—1357—

Find with other people
what cannot be found alone—
find alone what other people have done.

—1358—

To get unstuck from the muck unload a truck—
it's writers luck.

—1359—

The undisciplined artist is as useless
as the undisciplined athlete—
one lives to create and the other to compete.

—1360—

Cocaine is too easy to overcome pain
and the price too high for the brain.

—1361—

Beauty teaches itself in a *class*
of transcendent class.

—1362—
Inside the mouth is an eye
that sees whatever is said.

—1363—
Violence and silence
are on opposite sides of the fence.

—1364—
Sense and non-sense are both the same tense.

—1365—
The play of play is play.

—1366—
Sit *satisfied* after taking a stand.

—1367—
Musicians want to see
what they play visually in dance—
artists want to hear
what they paint in a trance.

—1368—
The new ritual is both actual and virtual.

—1369—
Paper covers stone, whether doll or tiger tone.

—1370—

Growing and knowing is what is showing.

—1371—

Though not in high command,
Incomplete man is in popular demand.

—1372—

An airplane has its own survival plan: flight.

—1373—

Grounded like a worm with a bird's eye view—
surge beyond the norm.

—1374—

Ray of Creation extends down
from highest elation to the lowest station.

—1375—

The world is of an age
to be played out on any stage.

—1376—

In the ultimate quest, there is no question of rest.

—1377—

Survive on verb and herb.

—1378—

Right ingredients are gradients of taste
that have no recipe.

—1379—

To slip or slide—need a guide to glide.

—1380—

App*ea*rance conceals the ear in its dance.

—1381—

Active power is an attractive flower.

—1382—

A fish with a cane is not blind
nor can it wait to take the bait off the hook
used to stroll down its brook lane.

—1383—

The sage *is* the message.

—1384—

When the perfect egg is laid,
the bill we owe our creators will have been paid.

—1385—

Truth in the nude is not always crude nor rude,
and may include clothes as prelude.

—1386—

Heart is needed for blood to flow
and art is needed for its flood to know.

—1387—

Play what you say and say what you play.

—1388—

Nature is naturally saturated with its own nature.

—1389—

Only when stumped does a branched-out tree
lose track of its trunk.

—1390—

Rotate on its axis is a spiritual praxis.

—1391—

A certain face may in space leave the earth's face.

—1392—

The secret of time
is not in the clock's chime
but in its vibration clime.

—1393—

Wearing planetary gloves
the giant boxer went global
in the universal ring of moves.

—1394—

Evolution of mankind:

cave, to house, to castle, to man,

to Mind.

—1395—

A flying fish strives for stardom

after seeing a *star*fish lying in its fallen kingdom.

—1396—

Be original—recreate the origin.

—1397—

It's not greed if to hoard truth is a need.

—1398—

Culture does not hide out back

nor live in a cul-de-sac.

—1399—

Happiness is not found anywhere—

it is everywhere around.

—1400—

The Word is the center of the world

when heard.

—1401—

Past loves to parade

in front of future as its own charade.

—1402—

Between the eagle and the vulture
soars an entire culture.

—1403—

Fantastic is not always fantasy.
Fantasy is not always fantastic.

—1404—

Pure beauty contains the impure for sure.

—1405—

Stillness is distilled noise—
chaos is disorder with no border.

—1406—

Reward moves forward, not backward.

—1407—

Leeches draw strength from long speeches—
laconic is not moronic, but iconic.

—1408—

Abstractions are energy subtractions:
Multiply visions and add to divisions.

—1409—

A true religious leader never speaks of religion.

—1410—
Ideally a control tower,
the mind has become a central train station
where one train of thought enters
as quickly as the other centers.

—1411—
A light reflected can be more luminous
than its original source—
a reflection of truth to endorse.

—1412—
A saint is not a new form to be born
but a unique color expressed in paint.

—1413—
Yield to the field: create!

—1414—
Successor of success
is not always progress but could be excess—
all part of the process.

—1415—
When belief happens all around—
sound is ground for relief.

—1416—
Turn your head and the world appears ahead.

—1417—

Knowledge is in the body—
a body of knowledge.

—1418—

Mine the field to find what the mind can yield.

—1419—

Can't write off writing—can't shrug the drug.

—1420—

There is no pleasantry in that sharp dividing line
between gentry and peasantry.

—1421—

Can't speak for the truth, it speaks for itself.

—1422—

Meaning cannot be magnified, only amplified.

—1423—

If God is the mechanic and we the car,
then who is driving?

—1424—

A flower is a *machine* manufacturing beauty
in its underground *plant*.

—1425—

Dig a deep well, learn a craft well—
all is well.

—1426—

Comfort is discomfort.

—1427—

A wise serpent is cunning,
shedding its old skin instead of *running.*

—1428—

Obstacles instruct more than obstruct—
they construct not to get stuck.

—1429—

Knowledge of the narrow ledge
decides what to pledge.

—1430—

Only zeal can keep it real.

—1431—

A great woman fills a man's heart,
a lesser one tears it apart.

—1432—

To produce a star, need to become one.

—1433—
Mistakes are made in fragmented states.

—1434—
Save her to savor.

—1435—
The core is easy to ignore.

—1436—
"Old moon" will not be back anytime soon.

—1437—
Blank paper needs the pen to thank.

—1438—
Aristotle is philosophy's categorical throttle.

—1439—
Wordplay is wisdom's foreplay.

—1440—
Cosmos made up God to create.

—1441—
Teachers are searchers, searchers are preachers.

—1442—
Language can gauge its own age.

—1443—

Vowel is not virgin—
it penetrates its own sound to howl.

—1444—

In the ideal monastery
they play the monochord
and worship the lord.

—1445—

Be the understudy: don't overthink.

—1446—

Express thoughts with a hammer
with little thought for grammar.

—1447—

Quantity and quality— perennial duality.

—1448—

Golden thread is well-read.

—1449—

Affairs of God are set up in pairs.

—1450—

To Know— *know* you do it.

—1451—

Quest for reality *is* its totality.

—1452—

Doors of the sanctuary are agape
to let knowledge from within escape.

—1453—

Dispel illusion, come to a conclusion.

—1454—

Whether from inside a cave
or outside its walls,
kindle the Imagination
in the darkness of its halls.

—1455—

Hierarchy without eros is chaos.

—1456—

The lamp shone on the creative bone.

—1457—

Wisdom *is* kingdom.

—1458—

"Drop" returns to its cloud
to shower its own lust for power.

—1459—

Don the creative frock
to turn on the write to unblock.

—1460—

Write longhand—a shorthand to understand.

—1461—

Professor professes to know;
student confesses it's all show.

—1462—

Booked and *sentenced* to finish the book.

—1463—

Drive the position in code
to listen to the vapor explode.

—1464—

Eye of the storm is a visionary norm.

—1465—

The void is trapped in a trapezoid,

—1466—

Dig deeper into its mine to map the mind.

—1467—

Home of the spirit is spirit of the dome.

—1468—

God forged a signature to steel our identity.

—1469—

In tempestuous weather
few have the strength to carry good fortune
as light as a feather.

—1470—

Reserve the unconscious reservoir, consciously.

—1471—

Capture genuine style not being in denial,

—1472—

Be reasonable!—
Reason cannot complete with Revelation.

—1473—

Bird sits atop the carved totem as unique item.

—1474—

Purpose of war is to show the complete loss
of sense of purpose.

—1475—

Miscommunication is common ammunition.

—1476—

Which is a more serious inflation:
ego or economy?

—1477—

Mass is created for the mass.

—1478—

Real theology is primordial mythology.

—1479—

States of illumination
or illuminated states.

—1480—

No leaning in meaning.

—1481—

Mythical kings had the ability to do many things.

—1482—

In romantic languages
love and hate are masculine,
while beauty and ugliness are feminine.

—1483—

Waves bathe the sand, thoughts bathe the brand.

—1484—

Hoorah for the Torah!

—1485—

The story the prospector told
is worth more than the gold sold.

—1486—

A Book of Philosophy does not have to be long
to find out where its words and thoughts belong.

—1487—

Seeing is *being* at the right moment.

—1488—

Tackle each shackle.

—1489—

Everything is as it is *and* nothing is.

—1490—

Channel is a narrow passage
to channel its author—the sage.

—1491—

Spinning is winning.

—1492—

The ship's aim to stay the course
is to claim authorship.

—1493—

The burden of boredom
is to carry around *nothingness.*

—1494—

Leaks are the enemy of peaks.

—1495—

Color-blind can't find the mind.

—1496—

Seek to peek at the peak.

—1497—

Imagination is real world stratagem
with no material substratum.

—1498—

Imagination is both hardware and software,
all in one to wear.

—1499—

Fate is its own template.

—1500—

Even if the end of the world is near,
it won't be this year.

ABOUT THE AUTHOR

David L. Laing is a visionary self-taught artist and writer currently living and working in Seattle, Washington. His works in oil, acrylic, watercolor, and pen and ink drawing have been exhibited in South America, the United States, and Europe.

David expatriated in his early twenties and headed for South America with no money, in hopes of finding or founding a "New Paris for artists." Two months later and thirty pounds lighter, he limped into São Paulo, Brazil, having traversed the entire continent overland, nearly ten thousand miles, surviving purely on his own wits and with the aid of a few helpful souls. David spent over fifteen years in Brazil writing, painting, and composing music.

Since his return to the USA, David has focused on book publishing of his own novels, art books, and compilations of his articles. Solar Codex: A Light Odyssey and Notes from the Milky Way are the first two volumes in the quartet of Cosmic Adventure novels. At present, he is working on the other two novels to complete the quartet and is preparing for publication many new books of drawings, articles, dialogs, plays, and screenplays. Most of David's written work is lavishly illustrated with literally hundreds of drawings, all hand-inked by him.

PURCHASING ARTWORK AND CONNECTING WITH DAVID L. LAING

ARTWORK

Drawings and paintings from David L. Laing's books and other themed collections may be purchased at his Cosmic Art Center page on ArtPal, www.artpal.com/davidllaing. His work is available as fine art prints, canvas prints, custom framed prints, and even mugs.

WEBSITE AND EMAIL LIST

Visit David's website at www.davidllaing.com. Be sure to join his email list to be notified about new book releases, new art collections, exhibits, and other new projects.

ARTSANA VIDEO AND YOUTUBE CHANNEL

Watch the video of David's art book, *Artsana, 35 Sacred Yoga Asanas Expressed Through Art*, at tinyurl.com/artsana-video. Produced by One Field Media, www.onefieldmedia.com, and David L. Laing, this short film features eight extraordinary yogis, accompanied with music by Andre Feriante, www.andreferiante.com.

See book trailers and animations of David's illustration on his YouTube channel, tinyurl.com/cosmic-art-center-videos

BOOKS BY DAVID L. LAING

ART AND COLORING BOOKS

Higher Glyphs

Artsana: 35 Sacred Yoga Asanas Expressed Through Art

Alpha 2 Zulu: Military Alphabet Coloring Book

AlphaBetter: Coloring Book of Letters and Numbers

Kolor Khmer

Ancient Runes: For Coloring and Meditation

Willing Evolution

Dance of the Dance

ANTHOLOGIES

ARTICLES

Beyond the Box, Volume 1

Beyond the Box, Volume 2

Beyond the Box, Volume 3 [Forthcoming]

Beyond the Box, Volume 4 [Forthcoming]

APHORISMS

Not Yet Human

Almost Human

Just Human [Forthcoming]

Fully Human [Forthcoming]

NOVELS

COSMIC ADVENTURE QUARTET

Solar Codex: A Light Odyssey

Notes from the Milky Way

Pentagram Rising [Forthcoming]

Prometheus Reforged [Forthcoming]